The 5 F Strategy

Bottom-line Growth in Any Economy Without Adding Sales or Marketing

Nola Heale

Protea Consulting Professional Corporation
Chartered Professional Accountant
Alberta, Canada

Copyright © 2020 by Nola M. Heale.

All rights reserved. No part of this publication may be reproduced, distributed or transmitted in any form or by any means, including photocopying, recording, or other electronic or mechanical methods, without the prior written permission of the publisher, except in the case of brief quotations embodied in critical reviews and certain other noncommercial uses permitted by copyright law. For permission requests, write to the publisher, addressed "Attention: Permissions Coordinator," at the address below.

Protea Consulting Professional Corporation
P. O. Box 74131 Strathcona
Calgary, Alberta, Canada, T3H 3B6
www.ProteaConsulting.ca

Ordering Information:
Quantity sales. Special discounts are available on quantity purchases by corporations, associations, and others. For details, contact the "Special Sales Department" at the address above.

To Tweety

Table of Contents

Business Success with Fun 1
1. Focus on the Drivers 7
2. Financial and Management Reports – the metrics 25
3. Feedback and Feed-forward – plan and strategy 41
4. Funds and Funding – secure in good times 53
5. Financial Management – creative value 67
6. Business Success, Value and Profit is Fun 81
7. Afterword – Top 10 Mistakes that Prevent
    Bottom Line Growth 89

Introduction

Business Success with Fun

Why do the statistics show that up to two in five companies (depending on the location in which they operate, industry and certain other factors) fail or terminate operations within the first three years from incorporation, half survive five years and only one in three see their 10th anniversary? These founders and managers spent a large portion of the time struggling, stressed and not enjoying the experience.

As the founder or senior management of a fantastic company on a mission to create, deliver and accomplish amazing things why does it sometimes, or regularly, feel so hard?

Every business founder and senior management executive strives to make their company group a raving success, an overnight success if possible! The success must be measured in all of profitability or return to all stakeholders, in achieving its purpose, and in the personal fun and enjoyment the people derive from the journey.

There are consistent themes when we contrast successful and failed, or struggling, companies. They include:

- Being acutely aware of the financial health of the company, or only periodic (or superficial) knowledge of the finances.
- Identifying successful and struggling areas in the business, and seeing early warning when a pivot is required, then taking appropriate action. Or managing the company as a whole in one combined report that is often available well after a period end (or at a financial year end only) when reaction would be late or of no effect.
- Setting and achieving realistic, although visionary, strategies and goals, or alternately working to achieve no regularly agreed strategy or set of goals.
- Cash and financing available at the right time to boost, or leverage, results. Or the company having difficulty funding growth (including during difficult economic periods).
- Consistently creating value in the business and for all stakeholders, which may include one of both of quality of earnings and transformation. Or continuing to operate the same business model.
- Focus on "fires of the day" activities or encouraging management, and potentially the entire team, to have periodic open, honest and impartial conversations and evaluations of "what we do, how we do it and what should we be doing".
- Fully empowered people with skills and experience that are the best and most appropriate for the job at the time in the company's lifecycle, or using people significantly outside of their area of expertise and requiring them to "make it work" in too broad a portfolio of tasks or roles for too long a period.

Thrive Despite and Because of the Business Environment

Businesses can, and should, survive *and* thrive irrespective of the general business climate. There are many examples of companies that were "ahead of their time", that struggled for many years on the road to success or that seemed to survive and succeed "despite themselves". For many it comes down to a stubborn determination to succeed, a willingness to change and learn, the right people and informed perseverance; some also partnered with or were mentored by a person who can appropriately guide and supply impartial evaluation.

The "magic bullet" is a combination of 'what' 'why', and 'who'.

Executives and owners who utilize strategic tools and partner with empowered, capable and enthusiastic team members see ongoing success, remain vigilant for signs that changes are required, and are humbled by achievements of the sum of the components. Economic conditions do not kill companies, the people working in, on and for them do. Harsh economic conditions create strong resilient, successful companies because those companies have devised the recipe for success.

Achieve Success

Ongoing sales and cash flow are critical for the continued existence of every business although they will be achieved on different timelines that may be influenced by industry, regulations, maturity of the technology or other factors specific to the company. As a society we need more diversity in successful companies; companies that achieve the required balance between returns, "fun" for their team, and enviable success. We need the competitive choice, the increased employment, the positive business environment and atmosphere that success creates, and to reduce the waste that financial loss and emotional pain bring when a business fails. Your business can be, and must be, one of the successes! You have the power to make your business supreme and unrivaled.

A small number of strategies and tools when implemented and maintained will create a stable springboard for exponential growth, save measureable amounts of management time, and at the same time inject fun and some good natured challenge and team-spirit into seeing the business progressing. Is your business on this path?

Harness Energy and Exhilaration

Among the most exhilarating times are those when your business is seeing success or a reason for rapid action. When a large profit is reported, when a client awards a large contract, when a significant patent or certification is received which supports expertise pricing and lucrative contract proposals, the team develops 'spring in their step'.

When bad news is received ...
- discovering a delay in commencement of a contract,
- a shortage of cash due to unexpected expenditures, delayed collections or funding grants,
- research and development extending beyond a critical deadline, or
- even a major change in economic or industrial environment,

most companies create an energetic flurry of activity to solve the problem or avert the risk.

The secret is to harness this energy and develop a motivated team that:
- continually fine-tunes operations,
- remains alert for opportunities or changes, and
- rises to meet challenges

such that the enthusiastic team spirit is the energy behind the success growing the business, increasing profitability and managing cash flows. The way to keep them enthusiastic and empowered is to create a support mechanism that keeps the team informed with minimum effort and thus immediately alert when action is required.

Value in Deliberate Discipline

Most companies that grow the fastest and survive the longest operate very deliberately and gather size-appropriate disciplines and processes to enhance and support their excellence. The most successful ones develop laser focus on detail of their own business and pair it with awareness of developments in their operating environment.

Business founders and executive teams often struggle to quantify the value of shared services (administration, accounting, human resource, etc.), investment in technology and security, and the time and effort required to standardize their processes and procedures. This is, at least in part, because there is no visible link to the sales process or profitability. Consequently these functions are often under-resourced, disrespected as "living only in the past", misunderstood, and considered to be a "necessary evil". The teams working in the functions, in turn, do not know how to demonstrate their value, and often emphasize rules over business practical, thus reinforcing the perception they add inadequate value and their cost is too high.

In contrast, in successful companies administrative or back-office teams efficiently partner with customer facing and operational functions to streamline processes, add automation to reduce workload and provide immediate feedback. The teams combine to become one integrated team that seamlessly provides all parts of the business service, and consequently remove significant cost, generate increased value and contribute to corporate growth.

How do they do it?

In this book we explore tools that can enable success and accelerate growth of your company. Implemented well and customized effectively they do not add costs, they create efficiency rather than bottlenecks, and they exponentially enhance the corporation's value and contributions. The tools may be used individually but are cumulative in effect, with most value derived when all are in use.

If your management wants to free up some of their time and cut costs these are for you. Most companies find they are already using one or more, at least in part, but those that comprehensively implement the full suite find they are the trigger to the exponential growth they desire.

Is your company ready to grow, have fun learning and using new tools, and enhance the experience for all of your employees?

"It is not the strongest of the species that survives, nor the most intelligent, but the one most responsive to change."
Charles Darwin

Chapter 1

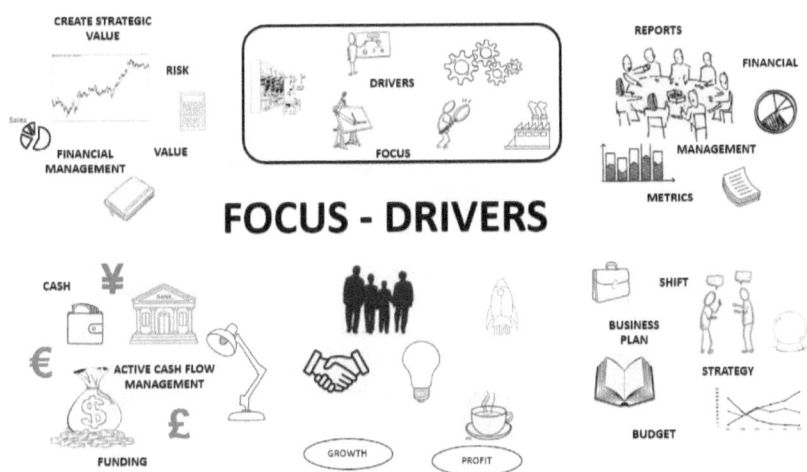

Focus on the Drivers

Bob[1] is the chief executive of a company supplying quality engineered, premium priced products and services in a highly regulated industry. He was promoted when the company was publicly listed, significantly in debt, had filed incomplete public documents and many believed had no chance of survival; employees were leaving in quick succession and the sales pipeline was slow to deliver results. In a few short years this company became the very profitable premium priced global leader of its market niche and underwent exponential expansion of facilities.

Sally[2] took an approach that was similar and yet very different in leading and assisting her large group of independent affiliated

---
[1] To protect the privacy of clients I have blended companies and situations into composites that give the realities without specific details of the engagement. Not his real name
[2] To protect the privacy of clients the specific names and details have been adjusted to present the realities without specific identification. Not his real name

companies operating in an industry struggling with low margins and extreme rates of violent crime. Through mentoring and targeted activities within her company and the industry she ensured they experienced multiple successes, increased their profits and expanded services, reputation and geographic reach.

The executives have very different styles and personalities, and their companies have few similarities. Yet they both strongly believe their focus on customized key business indicators and the view they provide to manage daily performance were a critical ingredient in the corporate turnaround and success.

Their companies continued expanding during industry contractions, global recessions, and even changes in their own shareholders, financing arrangements and corporate structure. Bob added two shifts in his factory, a new production line and moved to a second facility in a new country; Sue more than doubled the technical capacity and functionality of her affiliates, and the attacks on the vehicles almost stopped.

Bob and Sally's experience is very typical for many executive teams that manage their companies with the aid of carefully identified drivers they tweak and refine.

Seeing Progress

A business is successful when experiencing measurable progress. The core purpose is being achieved, the company is growing, stakeholders all see benefit, and investors appreciate the profitability and positive cash flow. Fiscally responsible management identifies ways to ensure their companies flourish so the creativity and innovation do not disappear.

To determine progress management needs a mechanism to measure performance and results so that the achievements can be *seen* daily and compared over time.

In the smallest companies the founder is aware of all that is happening and may watch the cash in the bank; that may be all that is required. But, as the company grows, and functions and tasks are delegated to the oversight of more people, it becomes necessary to formalize the measurement, reporting and team review of strategic metrics or reports. In this way management processes are efficient, everyone works to the same objectives, and early warnings are seen if something in their environment changes or they need to make business changes. The alternative is the place where too many companies find themselves, with inadequate success, no cash and a decision to cease operations.

Key Drivers – Why so specific? How Many? How to Identify?

Every company has a very small number of true drivers; things that when actively "steered" determine the precise level of overall success or failure.

They are critical to watch regularly (usually daily) and change behavior or activities to maintain or improve. (There are also a larger number of important, though less strategically critical, items that must be managed regularly which, for most companies, is in monthly or weekly more detailed reports (see Chapter 2).

The primary driver items must be identified very carefully. They are the *primary* drivers, the most critical or strategic determinants of success, or items that must be minimized or avoided to elude certain destruction or diverted progress. Inadequate effort in identifying drivers will waste valuable management time (spent managing something that does not driver performance, or in trying to manage too many measures), make no positive impact on performance or, in the worst case, actually drive failure.

Does Management Already Know?

The likelihood is high that your management already inherently "knows" what these items are. Your company can begin reporting and managing those. Or perhaps still formally consider options to be sure there are no additional, or more specific, drivers that had not been considered.

Some business so seldom comes up for air to re-evaluate what they are doing and how they do it, the mere exercise of thinking about the drivers will produce interesting conversation and a reality check to ensure internal factors (like processes, practices and structure) are not in fact hindering growth.

Make a Start. Don't wait.

Identifying the first primary drivers is always the most challenging! However, for long term survival and success it is a discipline that cannot be overlooked or avoided. Make a start! You can change or adjust over time too.

Procrastination is destructive. Once the drivers have been identified and measurements agreed the reporting and customization are easier. When everyone in the company understands them the observations and progress often become motivational "rallying cries" or team-spirit builders on the road of growth.

So what is a "Key Business Driver"?

Business drivers are elements that either build or protect the value of the business, or can easily destroy a company, or part of it. Defined another way, they are items or conditions that enable the company to become and remain successful.

A *key* business driver is one that is vital for the continued success and growth of a specific business; the "collection" or "combination" that initiate and support activities that will help the specific company define and accomplish its goals.

To identify the drivers to focus on, management must address two key questions:

- Which factors will have the most significant *impact* on the value of the business (and/or the specific strategic goal being considered)?

- Which of those factors can be most effectively *managed*?

Step into the Drivers - Goals to Drivers

Some of the most common strategic goals (in no particular order) are:

- increased shareholder value,
- business growth,
- product and/or service success, changes or improvements,
- market growth,
- growth or defense of market share,
- optimization of time to market,
- intellectual property development, protection, or increase in value,
- facilities, equipment and capacity increase, utilization enhancement, or reconfiguration,
- resources secured, alternatives, or utilization and improvements or enhancement,
- threat or risk identification, avoidance and/or management,
- the right people, people engagement and utilization,
- environmental factors and performance,
- social factors and performance,
- availability and efficient use of cash, financing and funding sources,
- technology utilization or improvement,
- enhanced value to various stakeholders,
- customer satisfaction,
- governance factors and performance,
- regulatory certification and maintenance of accreditation.

The 7 key business driver categories that are the most common are:
1. Profitability: Are we continuously driving revenue up and costs down?
2. Productivity: Are we producing our goods and services in a way that is ever-more efficient and effective? Are we using our people, facilities or resources well?
3. Time to market and defense of market: Are we moving from concept to sale fast enough to keep a competitive edge? Are we maintaining and growing in our chosen market and niche?
4. Customer Satisfaction: Are we making our customers happy enough to become and remain loyal fans?
5. Stakeholder Impact: Are we performing in a way that benefits stakeholders at all levels?
6. Cash flow: Are we generating or raising enough cash to operate and grow the way we plan?
7. Growth or strategic change and repositioning: Are we planning and executing the right activities to achieve the intended growth or to reposition the company at the appropriate time?

Agree which items are your company's strategic goals and hence driver categories. Now within those, identify *the* most important item (or sometimes two that compliment or are opposite) to measure and manage within each. Answer the question "What is the absolutely most important thing that will change this item?"

The quest for long-term business success and value starts with a clear understanding of the variables that significantly create or destroy that value or success, these are the *key business drivers*.

Identifying and managing specific targeted drivers helps management to focus on activities that have the greatest impact.

Now what? .... Measure and Share

To identify drivers the first time or where those identified previously are revisited or reconsidered, many companies action as a special project or have one person tasked to get the first discussion version prepared. These do not have to be time or cost intensive but create the focus that is necessary to get the task done both efficiently and effectively.

Once identified they must be measured and shared to those you can take action on them.

Measure what is controllable:

The way to measure the driver depends entirely on what the item is. Some drivers can be challenging to measure but management should not be discouraged; remain flexible to try alternatives if the first method or measure does not produce effective results.

A driver is only useful, and worth measuring regularly, if it is controllable or at least manageable by the business. If something is important due to its "impact" on the business but is not something management can influence it is not a driver and the company will want to consider two options:

    a. Monitor (and even report on) the item regularly and
        i. actively manage the company's response to the factor or situation and/or
        ii. the impact it has had on the business and
        iii. the go-forward plans, or
    b. Periodically report on the item for awareness but not track it as a managed item.

See the change:

Once the driver is identified management needs a way to "see" it. For most impact a "visual" presentation usually works best and ensures all users have the same understanding. Use a method that will work well for all users, can be effectively reported on a regular and timely basis, and is appropriate for the specific driver.

Alternative presentations that may be effective for each driver:
- A table of numbers
- A bar graph
- A line showing trend over a period
- A set of traffic lights (red/green/orange that depict areas of concern, warning, or on target performance.)
- Stacked bars or a pie chart

The graphic may need to be accompanied by a few effective points of explanation.

Example:

If the priority is "Make sure we have sufficient cash to operate efficiently for another year", and the most important factor to achieve that is "sell enough Widget A at the right prices", how do you measure and watch that total sales of Widget A are adequate? Perhaps track total value of Widget A sold and the average price per unit sold. Perhaps circulate those 2 numbers (or the trend and cumulative numbers of each) to all executives by email first thing every morning? and then perhaps in the monthly reports management will consider whether there are any factors "consuming" too much of the cash Widget A has generated.

If the priority is "Ensure products are produced consistently to ensure optimal quality and avoid excess cost", what is the most important factor to measure? Perhaps machine downtime? Perhaps track trends in machine uptime and utilization?

If the priority is "Grow sales in our new products to progressively replace mature ones", perhaps track unit sales and profits, and the trend therein, for each product. This may be a line graph so the narrowing of the gap between products is visible. Could even consider driving sales by product (or category), and profit margin (in order to ensure new sales are adequately profitable to replace the mature products' profit contribution in the way expected).

Report Format and Location

The format chosen for sharing the information is highly dependent on a combination of the culture of the company, preferences of the chief executive (or management), the sensitivity of the information, how complex the information is and if, or how, users can meet.

- A report heading is always recommended, and usually a "key" that labels the measures is included for clarity.

- Some information may be presented on the company website, intranet, bulletin boards, etc. so can be changed as frequently and quickly as a new version becomes available. This method is chosen for charts, statistics and information of interest and relevance to the company as a whole or at least an entire department or team. If the information is highly sensitive, competitive or confidential it should generally not be posted in more "public" locations (e.g. where it may be seen by visitors or people passing the office). This becomes an easy method for everyone to be constantly aware of the status of the driver.

- Information may be posted or circulated in a report only to users who are able to use the information.

- Information may be shared verbally, example at daily status or "stand-up" meetings.

- Certain information cannot, due either to its complexity, nature (e.g. confidentiality, strategic nature), or to regulation, be presented in a public format and so analyzed, distributed and/or discussed on a "need to know" basis only.

- Driver reporting is always more useful if not done in isolation – present it as a trend, or as a ratio, by comparison to a period, another statistic or another tool (e.g. budget), and as a chart, graph or metric rather than dollar values alone (unless the actual amount is important, useful, or necessary in which case most companies present both the dollar and a representation).

If one of the measures is, or turns, negative and/or delivers a result that was not expected, analyze the detailed components of the items measured to determine where the problem lies and why.

Management can then take timely, targeted action to address the situation.

Small Number and Specific Key Drivers

Your company has a very limited number of items that are imperative to manage. These must be identified specifically and meticulously managed. Primary drivers are particular to every individual company, there is no "one-size-fits-all" although there may be some similarity within specific industries or operating environments.

> *Examples:*
>
> *A retail (or business-to-consumer) company will monitor daily sales and margins but these may not be important for a construction company working large public infrastructure projects.*
>
> * * * * *
>
> *One company will focus on their total daily sales while another may be concerned with the split and trend between individual products, or their ratio of sales per square metre.*
>
> * * * * *
>
> *A start-up entrepreneurial company will watch their cash and cash flow daily while a well-established company with sales and cash receipts well ahead of the sale and with established debt facilities may instead manage a portfolio of investments, cash and borrowings.*
>
> * * * * *
>
> *Some enterprises are concerned with sales in a specific product – this may be the product that represents the largest value of their sales, or highest margin, or it may be sales in a product that is very niche to the company and hence strategic to look after and grow both the value of sales and profit on that one. For some companies the product sales will be inter-related while for others each sale is independent; some companies need to constantly*

> *monitor sales by location while for others a periodic review by location is adequate.*
>
> ** * * * **
>
> *Many manufacturing companies need to manage their daily output, or major raw material components - ensure appropriate amounts of material are on hand and confirm ongoing availability - as well as manage the cost. Some also must be sure of in-time supply and manage dependence on specific suppliers that could be a bottle-neck or risk.*

Maintain to Ensure Value is Derived

Once the key drivers have been identified and reporting commences the process will feel easier and should take little time to maintain and circulate, or continue. The important part is to ensure:

- Report regularly; on the schedule that has been agreed,
- Keep the report useful and used – if the drivers are no longer relevant or the report is not used stop preparing it (or change to something that is useful). It is important to manage resources and to respect all members of the company's team by insisting that time is only spent on work that is useful and important, and this includes that reports that are produced are used for at least their intended purpose.
- Review the drivers and measures periodically to ensure what you have identified remain the most important, accurate and strategic drivers for the business, and that the "way" they are presented and acted on remain appropriate and useful.

As the well-worn saying goes "what is measured is managed" so measure and manage the *bes*t key driver items and ensure they are helping to grow your business.

Companies on a cycle of analyzing, monitoring and intentionally driving their performance and status experience stronger, more predictable returns, and actively steer their growth. They:

- Are less frequently surprised or blind-sided by unexpected events or circumstances in their environment,
- Take earlier action to manage situations, circumstances, or events that do arise and
- Less likely to have to create a panic response, not least of which is on a shortage of cash to continue operations that is only identified when it may be too late to avert danger. It is never late to start tracking key drivers, and the process is continuous. If a previously profitable product or customer suddenly stops being profitable, or even ceases sales entirely, the successful company should be immediately alerted by the key drivers (or even have had early warning) and be able to pivot to a response so the business takes the appropriate action in good time.

Tailor the Drivers

Every business is different and internal and external factors affect the performance. The secret is to monitor a select group of appropriate drivers that truly are key and that are presented in a useful format.

Avoid
- Data dump (circulating large volumes of raw facts or statistics),
- Too many measures (because attention is too fragmented),

And
- Don't tie-up valuable staff and management time in too much deep ongoing analysis as that has a worse impact on the company than having no driver information. It distracts everyone from focus on daily business activity.

Consider
- That drivers can be interdependent so it may be necessary to track more than one (as the trends may be more meaningful), or to report the two together as a ratio or

statistic, or to carefully consider which one of the related items is actually the *primary*.

The secret is to focus on a handful of key drivers that:

- Have a major impact on performance and reflect progress of your business,
- Are measurable,
- Are comparable to a standard such as a budget, prior year's figures, a performance trend, or an industry average,
- Are actionable i.e. can be acted upon in order to change or maintain them.

Highly strategic companies regularly also report metrics that provide early warning e.g. the number of prospect enquiries gives an indication of potential future business (if the number decreases it could warn that the sales pipeline is less full and sales may be decreasing).

Think Laterally When Identifying Drivers

When identifying drivers for your company ensure that you and your team actively consider the possibility they may be "unusual".

Because a characteristic or tool (or combination of a few characteristics or tools) that drives a business is very specific to each individual company. Essentially the "secret sauce" that makes the company successful. It may be a combination of factors, circumstances and/or people at that point in time.

It may be something like

- the "chemistry" of specific people and/or the way they work together,
- the efficiency of particular equipment (which is difficult to explain as another piece of identical equipment does not produce as well), or
- the particular artistry and talent that an individual craftsman naturally applies in machining equipment parts.

Some of these are especially important to identify and manage appropriately .... And when it is a factor related to individual people it is critical to identify contingency plans to preserve success if, or when, the person can no longer be with the company.

Business excellence is very particular to a specific combination of factors and drivers at any particular time.

Optimize Focus

Meaningful and intentional prioritization is a certain springboard to success.

Tailoring

- the way people and resources are employed, or utilized,
- in areas that deliver the best value,
- that fully utilize the value of their ability or experience, and
- that progress the strategic corporate objectives

is an approach that never fails to deliver exponential success. It energizes everyone.

Determine needs, then fill the roles

It is especially important to avoid the mistake many companies make – do not design the company for the people, resources, opportunities or ability currently onboard. Identify the goals or objectives, and the drivers to manage to that success and then "structure" to achieve it.

Steps:
1. Focus on the success.
2. Find the best person, resource or tool for the job.

Where the current team members or resources are not what is required, change them. Move people to roles that fit them and utilize their talents best, redeploy or replace resources that are not fit for function, and where there are "unfilled holes" in the perfect design get it filled with a "new" person, asset or resource as necessary. The person may be new to the company or may actually be someone previously in an incorrect, or inadequate, role which is identified when you search for the skillset required for the task.

It is possible a true expert is required for some tasks and company growth or success. Get the expertise! Stay focused!

The world has become increasingly mobile and accessible due in part to electronic connectivity. It is usually possible to fill the exact need with the perfect person ... even if that person is on the other side of the world and potentially in a different time zone.

Use experts when it makes sense and pay only for the time and effort that directly contribute to your value and purpose. Professionals usually contribute well in excess of their "price" when properly used for their skill and experience. In many situations the company will be using people "full-time" when they fit the exact need but in other cases it may make more sense to obtain a limited commitment of time from each of a group of people required for their expertise. They will work "part-time".

- use senior people only for strategic or senior work, guidance or mentoring of team members, or creating and optimizing efficient processes and procedures (using them for "junior" functions is wasteful);
- use disciplined, diligent, hands-on people for transactional functions, supervision, and tasks with defined processes. These people produce exceptional quality in tasks that require time, efficiency and diligence (or in many situations these may recur periodically or be repetitive). But expecting them to achieve in functions well beyond their skillset creates frustration for everyone and the cost to the company is usually enormous.

Do not cut corners to use exclusively jack-of-all-trade generalists because specialists (or a person with the required experience) are usually significantly less expensive. They get the task done faster and without errors, the need for additional research, advice or supervision, etc. This springs the business forward sooner.

The secret of business, especially these days, is to focus relentlessly on your unfair advantage – the thing you do that others don't.
John Rollwagen, executive

NOTES

Chapter 2

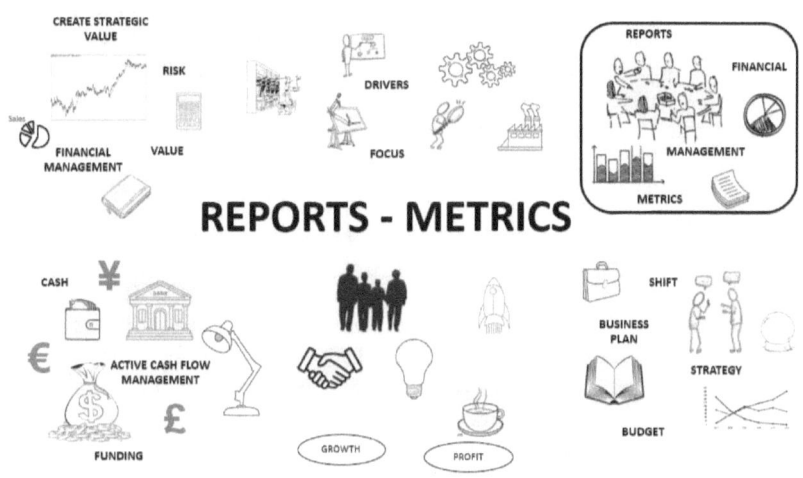

Financial and Management Reports – The Metrics

Evaluate Using Criteria, Reports and Metrics Specific to Your Company

To truly break a cycle, follow lean processes and achieve energizing but manageable forward momentum management needs a mechanism to measure performance and *see* the achievements. The drivers identified in Chapter 1 are watched regularly or continually (daily for many companies) because of their strategic impact on immediately changing the company, but it is as important to manage overall performance and trends.

Periodic reports for the business as a whole and for each major area within it provide a view of how all aspects are working together.

> *Step back and look at the total "where are we now", "how did it go" and "where are we headed."*

It is possible these reviews will reveal something additional that is a key or important driver to be added to the list (or substituted for something currently managed as a key driver). But the periodic reports and reviews provide their own value in the comprehensive integrated review of all drivers, progress, achievements and events combined.

> *Profitability is critical to a company's existence, but growth is crucial for long-term survival.*

Companies that have a cycle of analyzing, understanding and reacting to the performance and current status of the company experience stronger, more predictable, results, remain consistently profitable and achieve enhanced growth.

What Kind of Reports are Helpful?

The most valuable reports attempt to highlight the comprehensive performance of the entire company. They include statements and summaries extracted from the accounting records which are supplemented with reports on all departments, locations, functions, or components that will ensure users get a full understanding of the current status and performance of the business.

A good management report is not limited to information extracted from the account records. It includes information used to manage each individual, important function and aspect of the company.

Many companies prepare these reports to review the performance over the past month and compare that to forecasts and budgets previously prepared. It usually is meaningful to include trends into the past and future - most commonly the current year actual to date result, and that result projected forward for the next few periods or the balance of the financial year.

To prepare the first comprehensive reports (whether a new discipline or existing reports are being extended, changed or expanded) most companies use a "special project" or task one person to get the first version prepared. Once finalized the reports are easier to prepare on the agreed schedule (for most companies that is monthly) but the contents of the reports must be periodically reconsidered to ensure the items and way they are presented remain the most important, accurate and strategic.

Format is Guided by Use of the Report

The format of the reports is concise and effective so that managers and executives review them efficiently.

Many companies elect to meet monthly as a team to discuss the results, and agree targeted action plans and deliverables for the next reporting period. The duration of meetings and the report formats depend on the culture of the company and preference of the management. Some are very detailed while many are well summarized with all substantive further discussion occurring at smaller "sub-group" working-session meetings either before or after the top level meeting. Research has shown that meetings should ideally be no more than 60 to 90 minutes.

The discussions should include:

- Understanding the results themselves,
- Reviewing the interdependencies between factors,
- Discussion of ideas and strategies, or targets, to remediate or amplify performance and achievements. Progress planned for the next or future periods are usually also included.

Design and Tailor for the Company

As is the case with key drivers, management reports must be tailored specifically to the needs, preferences and focus of the company. It is not possible or desirable to design a "one-size-fits-all" as it will not target and highlight the specific areas that each individual company needs to focus on for growth. It certainly would waste resources in preparing information and reports that are not valuable for managing the company.

The financial and management reports may be designed as one for the company as a whole. Or they may best be designed as a summarized "top level" company-wide report (usually financial statements will be included at this level) and include most of the detailed analysis and information in supporting, subordinate reports for individual subsidiary companies, business units, locations or departments. Many enterprises find the detailed format is more meaningful for analysis and management.

Use and Remember

The report is both a tool for measuring and managing the company, and serves as a record of historic status and progress. Most companies regularly refer to previous management reports for comparative purposes or as a reminder of "what happened" in a period.

Companies that grow and achieve the fastest cannot preserve accurate records of the "state that was" in human memory. When an employee changes department or leaves the company any memory of events in the period is lost. Progress is only apparent in hindsight, management may not notice progress day by day, but if plans are followed, when progress is reviewed periodically in arrear the positive change is visible.

Your management needs to identify what reports you need in a comprehensive picture to know exactly what is happening in the company and see any warning signs.

Include What? Who Prepares it?

The financial information forms a core part of most management reports, and in many companies it is the finance and accounting team who prepare, or accumulate and distribute, the report.

However, a quality monthly management report must *not* be limited to financial information and certainly not "traditional format" financial statements only.

Financial statements show the results at a point in time and for the period, but the additional information gives more meaning to *why* those results are as they are and what can be expected to occur in the next period. The financial statements in combination with detailed reports and metrics (as applicable) lend colour to explain the significance or meaning of, and justify the interrelationship of, various amounts shown in those numbers.

1. Key Business Areas

Comprehensive management reports will include a range of reports, metrics, charts and information for each of the primary business areas, as are relevant to the specific company:

- operational or operations,
- customer pipeline and customer relations,
- manufacturing,
- supply chain,
- human resource,
- investor relations,
- quality,
- innovation, and
- technology.

2. Meaningful Inclusion of Time Periods – Report to a Current Date and the Month End

The additional information will very often be presented to a date within the last week because current information is necessary for effective management. But, the financial statements take longer to finalize and are usually presented to the last month end (perhaps two weeks after that month end, and hence already half way through the next month)

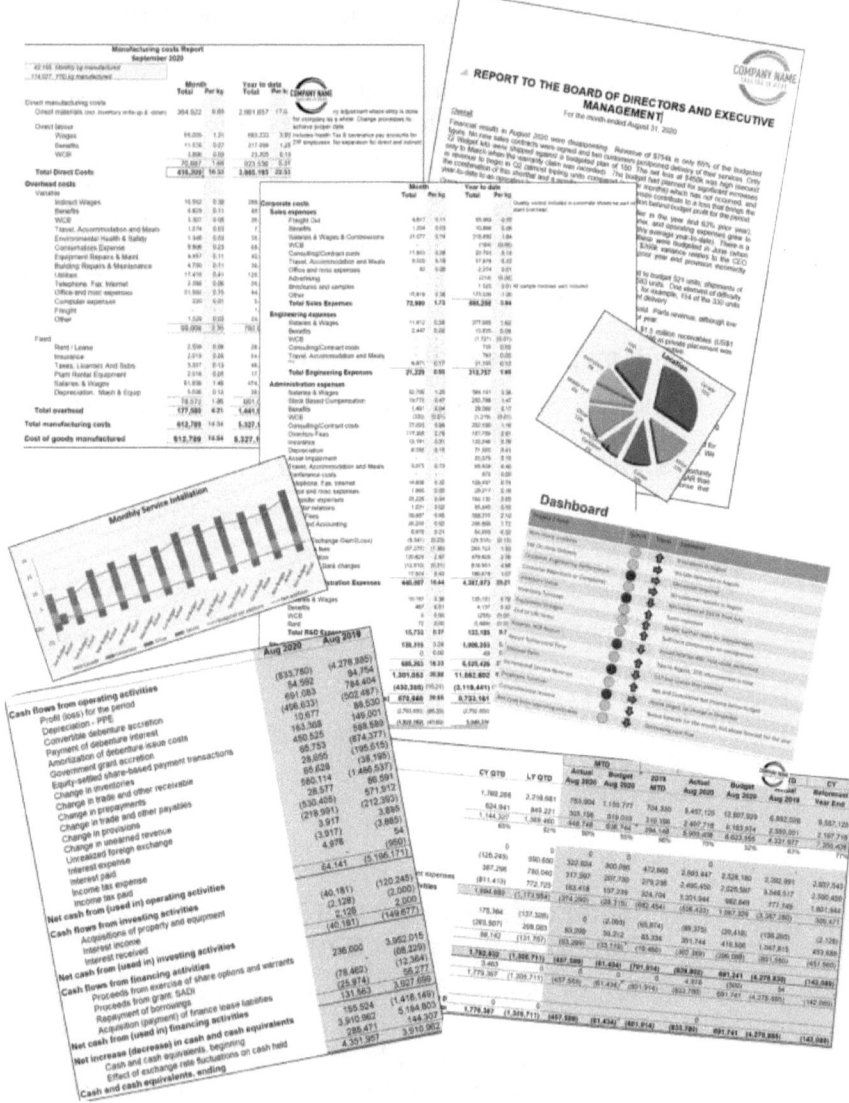

Even the accounting team should be required to present reports that are current where the information is useful for management – examples include outstanding accounts receivable, current payables (especially when the company has stringent cash flow management), project spending and/or revenue reports, etc. The more out-of-date management information becomes, the less valuable it may be. It is difficult to react to correct a problem or to enhance good results when it is well after the fact.

For managing the company effectively it is imperative to have past, current and near-term future information. The reports will often be accompanied by concise written comments to draw attention to key matters and/or provide explanation. The total set of information included in the report must give a comprehensive "picture" of the state of business, what progress has been made over the period, highlight both successes and areas of concern, and provide an update on initiatives or projects underway.

Information Considered for Inclusion in Management Reports

The components of your particular reports will be very specific to the company. This section lists many of the most common information usually included.

Most reports include as many of the following as are *relevant* and *significant* to the specific company. The components of the report may change between periods when an item is only relevant at a particular time:

- Summary financial statements (or if more appropriate or required by the CEO the complete balance sheet, statement of profit or loss, and statement of cash flow in traditional format).

    When a complete balance sheet, statement of profit or loss (or income statement as many prefer to call it) and cash flow statement in included be careful to ensure all recipients can understand and use the information.

Financial statements are easily misunderstood due to their technical nature and the requirement to comply with generally accepted accounting standards.

- Results of performance in key areas:
    - Sales or revenue analysis by major products, locations, departments as are relevant,
    - Operating or sales margins (i.e. total sales after the cost of sales and expenses directly attributable to selling the products or services), usually also by major products, locations, departments as are relevant.
    - Specific major operating expenses or groups of expenses that are relevant and material (e.g. salaries and wages, sales and marketing, rent and accommodation, maintenance, unusual expenses, innovation spending, etc.)
    - Funding costs (e.g. interest paid, penalties)
    - Net profit analysis often by location, or other subsections of the company or entity.
- Sources and uses of cash – information in an easily reviewed format of the large categories of items that have moved cash into, or out of, the company in the period.

    Review what is creating cash and what is using the cash.

    Is something producing impressive quantities of cash? It should possibly be monitored as a driver.

    Is something absorbing a lot of cash? Should it be, or does something need to change? and/or should it be managed with drivers or frequent reporting so problems can be identified quickly and/or so improvements can be identified fast, and then attempts made to ensure they continue.

- Major assets and liabilities:
    - E.g. inventory, receivables, payables, prepayments or liabilities accrued.
    - Usually reported in dollars, trends in value and sub-categories over time.

- - Any significant adjustments or allowances made to reduce the values to a "fair value".
- Major funding sources, when important:
  - Bank or other borrowings, grants and government funds, equity raised.
  - Often reported showing amounts received, amounts anticipated, facilities available or used, comments where applications have been filed for new funds.
  - Any other information useful to a comprehensive understanding of how the business is funding the future.
- Customers:
  - Metrics and charts related to customer delivery, service, and collections.
  - Examples:
    - Collection periods, day's sales outstanding.
    - Bad and doubtful debts.
    - Results of customer surveys.
    - 5 to 10 largest customers (to show dependence on key customers) by invoiced value, margin and collections.
- Inventory (where relevant as a major asset, when the company manufactures items, or when important for the way the company services their customers):
  - Metrics on total value, and splits by major categories or components.
  - Inventory turnover.
  - Slow moving or redundant items and/or value and provisions.
  - Strategic products held (or needed), sometimes analyzed for key or strategic suppliers.

- Payables (especially when low on available cash):
    - Metrics on total value, split by major categories and/or products and/or locations, etc. as applicable.
- Metrics showing payment terms and/or aging – values currently payable, overdue or paid ahead of terms, deposits and prepayments paid before delivery, etc.
    - Day's payables outstanding.
- Quality performance and certification metrics and reports.
- Key or core operating progress, achievements or challenges e.g. if the company builds assets that are time sensitive, is working towards a major delivery deadline, is limited by seasonal characteristics, sees the impact of a major unexpected event, etc. then, what relevant charts, reports or comments need to be included?
- Major projects underway – relevant information and reports.
- Labour or employee hours, productivity, head counts, attendance statistics, results of satisfaction surveys, and various relevant ratios and qualitative information (including union matters, etc.).
- Production and/or man-hours, throughput, average cost, waste or scrap, capacity utilization, etc.
- Delivery targets and achievement, order backlog and/or pipeline, time to manufacture, etc. (by both time and value).
- Business development pipeline and sales, and business development reports and metrics.
- Investor relations information.
- Ratios or metrics that may be required to show relationships between other individual business measurements and metrics.
- Metrics and representations of loan, share, grant, etc. compliance e.g. compliance with covenants.

As much of the information as possible should normally be presented as charts, ratios, trends or other "picture" means that are easily understood at a glance by all required reviewers and users. These do not leave understanding to interpretation, all reviewers get the same "message" from a chart or similar.

The reports should, where possible and relevant, compare to the budget when available, and depict trends or progress, and comparisons.

Review and Use the Information Produced

1. Presentation and Distribution of Reports

The chosen report format is highly dependent on a combination of the culture and preferences of the company and management, how complex the information is, the sensitivity of the information, and if, or how, users can meet to discuss the reports.

- A report may be produced and posted or circulated only to recipients who are able to use the information.
- A meeting may be scheduled at which the report presentation is discussed, actions agreed and plans agreed for the next period. The measures and reports may be circulated before the meeting or seen for the first time at the meeting.
- Certain information is more valuable if it is obtained "immediately" it becomes available – example many companies look at daily sales and cash flow reports. These reports are more comprehensive than the driver reports per Chapter 1 but important to review regularly.
- Certain information is good if reviewed periodically either because it takes more time to accumulate 'useful' information or the type of information makes more sense periodically (e.g. a customer survey may only occur periodically; a rent expense or salary expense by day may not be useful if it is a flat amount each month).
- Certain information cannot, due either to its nature (e.g. confidentiality, strategic nature) or regulation be presented

in a public format and would be analyzed, distributed and/or discussed on a "need to know" basis only.

- Management reports are always more useful if presented as a trend, or as a ratio (e.g. sales expense as a percent of total revenue), by comparison to budget, forecast or a prior period, and, for some, as a chart or graph rather than dollar values. In some situations a "key" must be included on charts so users can understand what is represented, and a brief comment or explanation may be useful. A heading is always recommended.

- A summary of information may be presented on the company website, intranet, bulletin boards, etc. where informative for a large group of employees.

2. Discuss and Understand the Reports

Use Them

Monthly reports that are produced and only circulated to users by email (or as a printed report) are very often not read or used by the majority of recipients. Either because

- They are too busy and forget to review (they have the best intentions but time gets away and they forget),

- Because they review only select portions that are relevant or of interest to them personally or their department, or

- Because they do not understand information contained therein and don't have time or are embarrassed to ask someone for help or training.

Companies where the management team discuss their reports in-person in focused meetings achieve the exponential growth, hold more productive meetings, and develop exceptional team support and spirit across departments (which also facilitates those achievements).

A metric that appears to indicate a problem in one area usually has a cause and effect in different areas as well, without the individuals always knowing. When jointly discussed the rectification, growth or improvement happens together.

Most highly successful companies do meet to discuss their reports. There is a reasonably reliable link between frequency of discussion and the growth trend. Those that discuss monthly have higher growth than those who meet quarterly because trends can change suddenly in a three month period but, depending on the industry, meeting at least quarterly will facilitate consistent growth and value generation.

Focused Discussion

Discussion groups must be focused:

- Include enough people across all functions to allow for meaningful discussion and explanation of the reports,
- Guard against having meetings attended by too many people. These limit opportunity for discussion and full understanding, for developing action plans, or for celebration of successes and identification of early warnings.
- Avoid allowing meetings to become too long or unproductive. In larger teams, or companies, the reporting and discussion of the detail will often be in meetings at departmental, rather than company-wide, level. That is where team members can impact or react to or change the results. At the group, head office or senior executive level discuss less of the detail.

Company-wide Preparation and the Motivation derived from Management Reports

Companies that have an experienced senior controller or chief financial officer may use their guidance for the preparation process, alternative report layouts and measurements to include, and for further interpretation of the results and trends. It is not however essential to have senior financial team members because gathering the information and preparing the reports on a timely, consistent basis is a company-wide responsibility.

The financial team may co-ordinate distribution of the combined report. It is however the assistance and cooperation of all departments that makes the reports most meaningful, and the activities and progress effective in delivering consistent results that move the company towards accomplishing objectives.

The companies mentioned in Chapter 1 used their management reports, the key drivers, the achievements celebrated, and the need to address periodic problems or challenges, as team motivators that unified their teams and made them successful.

"Put it before them briefly so they will read it, clearly so they will appreciate it, picturesquely so they will remember it and, above all, accurately so they will be guided by its light."
Joseph Pulitzer, Editor

NOTES

Chapter 3

Feedback and Feed-forward

Manage with Purpose: The Right Strategic Focus

Management usually has most fun when they start dreaming and plan their progress for the road to greater success. From Chapters 1 and 2 the key drivers and management reports lay a solid foundation and team members gain enthusiasm from understand what is happening in the company; growth becomes increasingly consistent and predictable.

The key driver metrics and management reports can now be expanded to facilitate and manage driving the future. The drivers set the priority statistics and characteristics that describe the future successful organization. The results in the management reports allow business planning and steering through a feedback-and-feedforward process.

Current Known Facts Inform the Stretch

In order to move forward start with a high-level look at the current status and trend; how is the business doing in total, and each component, product line, department, branch?

- What is the revenue and profit trend looking like in each one?
- Is it stable, ramping up or slowing down?
- Where will that trend take the business if you project it into the future?
- Consider "non-numerical" facts and knowledge
    o Is it a growing or shrinking industry and/or market?
    o Is it, or should it be, premium or discount priced?
    o Is the cost and availability of inputs or overheads a problem?
    o What strategic changes are expected in the next 3, 5 and 10 years? (The company must consider the impact of those now in order to be poised to take advantage.)
    o Does the company want to continue operating in the same industry, or niche? Does it intend to be a market maker or a market taker?
    o Does the company need to, or plan to, develop a new product and/or service?
    o Etc.
- Where does management strategically want the business to be in a defined time period – 1, 5 or even 10 years?
- Are there additional environmental factors (economic, business, social, regulatory, or natural environment) that will have an impact on the business as a whole or some components?
- What strengths, weaknesses, opportunities or threats in the company, competitors, industry, market, customers, regulations, etc. should be developed or changed?

Future Changed or Accepted

Discuss and agree whether management plans to manage to the evolving future, with minor adjustments as become necessary, or intends to actively change the direction or progress and drive to a desired future. Is the plan even to change entirely, radically, e.g. move to a new product, service or industry?

If teams are enthusiastic and engaged they automatically stretch to go further, faster and prove that what others thought impossible is easily attainable. Instead of asking "why must we do that" they ask "why not achieve it and more". The team is the secret to success. The success and achievements themselves become the reward and drive the enthusiasm to perpetuate the cycle.

The key drivers and management reports provide understanding which empowers everyone and creates certainty and trust. The momentum and intentional activity in the desired areas combine to make your company remarkable, with a consistent understanding and ability to use that knowledge for objectives, plans and results in the next period.

Strategic Shift

As progress is made, management may decide to actively change and reengineer for intended strategic shifts. New business lines, new products, opening or closing of locations. Significant strategic initiatives like acquisition of additional companies (or operating assets or units), disposal of companies (or operating units) or restructuring of the business.

The Results are the Starting Point. The Sky is the Limit.

The results and metrics now become the starting point to plan and strategize for the short, medium and longer term. Most businesses create a detailed budget for a year and a strategic plan for 3 to 10 years.

The strategic plan should be a qualitative (not merely quantitative) exercise of planning and strategizing where the company is going on its current course, where management and the board want to take it to, and exactly how they plan to achieve those objectives. When there is a major event that creates significant uncertainty in the environment it may be necessary to adjust time horizons but the discipline and process usually remain.

Not a Badge or a Distraction

Most companies have prepared one or more of a business plan, strategic plan, or budget in the past but not all prepare them regularly. The process and discipline in the thinking and strategy are where the ongoing success originates for the business that survives for the long term.

An important rule is to not indulge in either extreme of:

a. Engaging in the exercise for the sake of doing it (and place a document on a shelf like a trophy), or
b. Allowing the planning and strategizing process to occupy people full-time for an extended period as they strive to achieve absolute accuracy and perfection.

Accept that planning tools must be well performed to be of value but, by their nature, are not perfect or 100% accurate. Expect plan and strategy detail to deviate from the actual results that occur, and perform comparisons in order to confirm that the course and results shown by the sum of the parts remains as intended.

> *It is especially important to guard against a failure to manage current business while preparing plans.*

Business Plan - Strategic Plan – Budget: Related, Connected and Progressively More Practical.

But What is the Difference?

The documents have overlap but serve different purposes and have very distinct features:

Business plan – answers the question "what does the business want to do or achieve? Where does it want to go?" It frequently includes an operational plan, marketing plan and financial projections. Often the business plan is among the documents given to lenders or funders to explain the business and what its objective is.

Strategic plan – answers the question "how will we do it? How will we accomplish what is set out in the business plan?" Usually includes similar information to the business plan (often in more detail) and a reasonably detailed action plan for the next 3 to 10 years. Strengths, weaknesses, opportunities and threats should be identified, along with a market, niche and/or competitor analysis, (and a summary is often included in the business plan).

Budget – answers the detailed questions
- "Which of the strategic plan milestones will we achieve in the next year,
- how much (in units and value) will we sell, spend, or do,
- how many and what skills of people do we need,
- what will the cash in and outflows look like, and
- how much are we going to spend on assets, research and strategic initiatives
- in the next 12 to 18 months?"

It is usually a month-by-month analysis in reasonable detail, in a format at least similar to the monthly financial statements (which then facilitates comparing actual results to the budget).

Living Documents

The plans and budgets must not be prepared and "forgotten". They are living documents and must be used, reviewed, reconsidered and revised.

Employee Buy-in

To derive maximum value and growth impact from the budget (which should be considered to be a more detailed first year portion of the strategic plan) the full management and employee team needs to "buy in" to it. Ideally they were part of the preparation process and they own performance toward ensuring objectives are achieved.

Strategic Adjustments

When your company is experiencing success and enthusiasm it is likely management will revisit the plans. In nimble high growth companies new opportunities may be identified and added to the original objectives. Be careful they are within the original strategic objectives or that the strategy is revised if they have been fully considered and are desired edits.

Assess if still on the same course, make corrections if there are unintentional detours or divergences (and the original course remains valid) or, in many cases, revise the plans when achievements begin revealing new, preferred, strategies and desired outcomes. In many cases the teams reach higher and faster.

Compare Actual and Budget Results

Budgets should be compared to actual results at least monthly and most companies, at least larger ones, revise the budget during the year (usually quarterly or mid-year). If there are any large expected differences (e.g. within two months of the year commencing sales are already well ahead of budget, or the business has found that plans to move into a new market were expedited so there are new activities, expenses and/or revenue) revise so the budget does not lose its purpose.

The "revised budget" will project, or forecast, what results are now expected to be for the financial year. The revised version is called a 'forecast', or a 'quarterly forecast'. A true budget should be prepared before the beginning of the year and kept unchanged for the full duration. Revisiting the budget is a very healthy exercise for the business and usually serves to keep revenue, expenses and cash flows within expected parameters and ratios.

Avoid Moving Goal Posts

Be diligent to avoid the temptation to "change direction" frequently. Like trying to catch a squirrel, the goal is elusive, the destination keeps changing and it becomes frustrating when little real progress is made. A company leader who does not stick to an objective long enough to allow team members to implement creates rapid loss of motivation because the team remains in a permanent planning mode, trying to change all of the time.

Represent in Numbers but *not* a Numerical Exercise

Although the budget and strategic plan do need to be represented in "numbers" they should not be a numerical exercise. The qualitative strategizing and decision making performed by management that determines "where" the business wants to go, "what" it will achieve and "how" it will do it are the most important parts of the exercise.

Perform the thinking, strategizing and descriptions first, and then represent in the required numerical format.

The chief financial officer, or senior financial person, assisted by other members of the finance and accounting team should be able to work with functional managers to represent the plans in a detailed projected balance sheet, income statement, cash flow and metrics (to include at least the ones that are used for the key drivers). They can then confirm that the plans of one team correlate with those of other teams.

The Budget is Valuable - Prepare and Use it Carefully and Comprehensively

Foundational Assumptions – Zero Based

The most valuable budget is built from foundational assumptions (e.g. what are the sales projections, or what research and development progress is needed, in this year to attain the agreed strategy). This method allows everyone to justify why every expense item is required and how each revenue amount is expected to arise.

The budget numbers are created from the facts by cascading out for the costs of earning the revenue, required business expenses, assets, funding, etc. to achieve those objectives. This form of a budget is often called a "zero-based budget" because it is designed to question or justify the need for all costs and ensure linkage where one item depends on another; it may take more time to prepare.

Year-on-year Approach

The alternative approach that takes the budget and/or actual results for the current year and considers the changes that should be made to derive a budget for the next year, is more traditional. The disadvantage of this method is that it does not facilitate fresh thinking about what is planned and why.

Monthly Detail and Adequate Detail

Monthly budgets that show the build-up of results over the year are more useful than one budget for the full year. However do not be tempted to prepare an annual budget and split into 12 even months. Every business has seasonal variations, projects or sales campaigns that commence or end part way through the year, people who may be employed part way through the year or only for a certain portion of the year, etc.

The costs, revenue and cash flows never occur evenly through the year and should not be budgeted that way. Also be careful to strike a balance between creating a budget that is too detailed and one not detailed enough. A separate budget for every item of revenue or expense in your business is not any more useful than having a budget that is only a select few large grouped categories.

Dependencies and Related Items

While preparing the budget or strategic forecasts remain vigilant for items that are related – similar to possibly needing batteries when you purchase a calculator, one expense or revenue item may necessitate another. As a result, sometimes you have to be careful not to change one line item of your budget without analyzing the effect the change may have on other line items.

For example, if you find that you are increasing your workforce by 10%, instead of simply increasing the payroll line item by 10%, you will want to increase employee benefits, payroll taxes and other items directly related to payroll. You may also need to consider additional personal protective equipment, work stations and refreshments.

In a similar way, if you increase your bottom line by increasing sales by 10%, don't forget to also increase variable costs related to sales (e.g., costs of goods sold, commissions, taxes and freight).

Consider Income Statement, Balance Sheet and Cash

A comprehensive budget should consider the impact on both the income statement (or statement of income) and the balance sheet. Prepare a cash budget as well as the well-known revenue and expense projections. Be cautious to utilize realistic cash flow timing:
- Time allowed for the anticipated or normal collection periods after sales are made,
- Timing of when you pay expenses will vary by the nature of the expense - salaries are within the month worked, perhaps you pay some expenses in advance (e.g. rent on the first day of the month or insurance annually in advance), and some expenses have payment terms so can be paid later.
- Allocate appropriate cash required for projects that may not generate results in the income statement.

The timing of cash flows will have a profound impact on the success or difficulties of a business, especially when it is expanding and growing. The cash budget will often identify problems before they occur or illuminate errors in other areas of the budget. Its greatest value is in identifying when it may be necessary to raise funds in the form of loans, grants or equity, or even to place an overdraft facility to bridge cash flow variation through the month.

Transparency of the Budget

A company's budget should not be a secret. There are instances when some financial information should be kept to a limited group, but general experience is that sharing the budget process, or at least sections thereof, with a wide group leads to greater transparency, increased feedback, beneficial communication and enhanced performance. Often the employee performing a task is the best informed person to be able to suggest what is possible or expected, or where improvements can be made.

After completing the preparation, review the budget and forecast to consider if it appears to be realistic and can be achieved in that manner and on that timeline. The higher the quality of the plans the higher the likelihood it is achieved, ensuring everyone stays on course and continues to build momentum and enthusiasm.

Resist the temptation to make "top level" adjustments to reduce costs and/or increase revenue. This can inject errors (not least of which is when related components are not all changed) and destroy morale.

It is more constructive to:

- Discuss and confirm the inputs, or foundational facts on which it was built,
- Consider if errors were made,
- Consider if perhaps the business plan or strategy will be achieved on a different timeline,
- Agree whether a "worst case", "likely" or "best case" basis should be used.

The budget and strategic plan are a "picture" of how well the team wants the business to grow in the year. When fully supported by everyone they very often elect to make the budget realistic and stretch but not unachievable. They acknowledge when the current trends are allowing for excellence or placing the company on an undesirable path. The team will recognize along the way when new opportunities present themselves that they want to explore, and that may be intentionally considered for inclusion in the budget or strategic plan (or to replace a current plan).

Goals are like magnets. They'll attract the things that make them come true.
Tony Robbins

Expect the best. Prepare for the worst. Capitalize on what comes.
Zig Ziglar

NOTES

Chapter 4

Funds and Funding - Secure Them in Good Times

Cash is Critical to Survival

Every business needs access to adequate, flexible and cost effective cash to survive and thrive. As Warren Buffet says "Cash ... is to a business as oxygen is to an individual: never thought about when it is present, the only thing in mind when it is absent".

Most new entrepreneurial companies are initially funded by the founder, sometimes with investment from friends and family, and potentially with debt facilities secured on the founder's assets. After that most companies require access to finance facilities or additional equity in order to grow.

Unless operating in an industry or niche where customers can quickly be secured in large enough, consistent, numbers and/or in some cases, where customer payments are collected ahead of the service or supply, new funding is required to continue operations and for strategic growth.

Explore funding alternatives and consider options *well before* the need becomes urgent. In many cases it will take at least six months to secure new cash.

Active Cash Flow Management

The best insurance for optimal performance is to actively manage working capital and cash. The availability and consumption of cash are an excellent window to the health of a thriving business.

Management that maintains excellent awareness of the ongoing cash in- and outflows, and who reviews a cash projection frequently take timely action to avert shortages and to optimize working capital management. The frequency of the cash projections should be adjusted between daily, weekly or monthly according to the volume of cash being used and the relative size of cash capacity (the combined total of available cash reserves and borrowing facilities).

Is All Cash Equal?

The three ways to get extra cash into the business (outside of business transactions) are borrowing, obtaining grants or by selling equity in the company.

The cost, funding terms or periods, contract terms, risks, security, and complexity vary significantly between different kinds of funding instruments. Not all options are available to every company or in every market, and many options are very unattractive in certain operating circumstances.

Funding is a complex topic with many variations and nuances so consider obtaining assistance or advice. The better informed management is the more advantageous for the company.

Forecast and Strategy Alert

The strategic plan, budget and forecast will warn of the need to raise funds. If planned growth, expansion or strategic initiatives reveal a need for additional funding the executive and financial management can begin exploring opportunities in adequate time. Even a change in operating conditions (e.g. customers start to pay slower, or supplier payment terms change so bills are paid earlier) can mean the company needs new cash to fund their working capital.

If management uses the forecasts to highlight a need to obtain cash they can ensure it is available when required, without a panic which distracts attention from improving and growing business.

The projection of cash, equity and funding requirements are undeniably among the most important outputs of the budget and strategic planning exercise. It takes substantial time to negotiate new facilities and it is much easier, and less stressful, to raise when cash is not yet required.

Remember the feedback loop into the budget: When new facilities are considered, ensure the covenants are modeled into the budget and forecast models on all probability scenarios (most likely, worst case, and better case). Management is then aware of the options or consequences if actual performance differs from the plan.

There may be options to repay or terminate earlier if that would be beneficial; in the worst case if management has reviewed the model "what-if" scenarios they know the risk if actual profits and cash flow are different to the plan. They know the operating results required for the company to stay on-side the loan, or grant, agreement and covenants, and hence can ensure strategies allow the required flexibility.

Gather Information and Confidently Solicit Funds

Raising funding, whether simple loans or something more complex can feel very intimidating as the terms used are all unfamiliar, many people have an aversion to "ask" for things and certainly do not want to reveal a need for help. There is uncertainty on where to commence the process because of the variety of options available.

Do not let fear deprive your business of essential funds which will prevent success!

There are many sources of assistance; make a start and you will find that even lenders and investors will make suggestions on other providers and vehicles to consider. (Many finance agents will work with the company to source appropriate funding as well.)

The information in the reports and documents that management uses to manage the company (management reports, budgets, strategic plans and business plans discussed in earlier chapters) can be used as the starting point in the funds negotiations.

Most lenders will require a full understanding of

- What the company does,
- How it plans to be successful,
- The funds required and for what period, and
- The profits and cash it expects to generate when the objective is achieved.

Management may want to present a different format, or a different quantity or depth of information, but the information required should largely be available through the business reporting process. The availability of the reports, and hence speed with which information can be supplied to the potential lender or funding parties, demonstrates that your company operates with good disciplines and governance. You are likely to receive the necessary funds with less effort and often at lower cost than a less prepared company.

Sharing Confidential Information

Always remain aware that when raising funds management is sharing confidential internal information and reports with parties outside of the business. Be careful to share circumspectly, obtain non-disclosure agreements where appropriate and in compliance with the policies of the company, and ensure you comply with regulations and legislation at all times.

Borrow and Court Investors When Cash Is Not Required

It may sound insane to ask for funds when the company has cash in the bank. But, it is always less expensive and easier to raise funding when the company has no need for funds. Raising finance (whether equity, debt, a hybrid, grants or several facilities) well in advance of the need will allow management to continue focus on operations and still be successful; it is less stressful and less expensive.

Grants must be awarded before the project commences and usually require matching funds from another source. So also consider applying for grants ahead of the project commencement (and simultaneously continue soliciting funding from other sources).

Begin speaking with investors and/or lenders when your forecast indicates growth *may* require more cash than will be available internally.

Consider the options when you

- Do not believe additional cash will be required but wish to consider options to establish what is available in the market, and the potential cost if external funds are obtained. You do not have to accept any loans or cash that is offered until you need it, or ever (and offers are always slow to arrive anyway). Or
- Have time to explore options and potentially obtain a blend of borrowing rates and terms before the forecasted need arises (this allows the luxury of speaking with many potential lenders or investors, and potentially securing several facilities).

If facilities are in place, or close to secured, before they are required management can focus on the strategic initiatives and business activities (raising finance is distracting at all times but even more so when it is essential for survival).

It may feel wasteful to pay a small commitment fee to keep a facility waiting unused. There are however many companies that truly believe the "unnecessary" facility or agreement was the springboard to tremendous expansion because it was available when an opportunity presented itself. Some companies have avoided bankruptcy because they had a "cash flow insurance" waiting when unexpected circumstances struck.

It takes substantial time to get new facilities in place and it is much easier and less stressful to raise when cash is not required. Funders are eager to invest when returns look excellent but very few will help when the company is under duress.

Review Terms and Clauses Carefully - Model Them in the Budget and Forecast

When new facilities are raised, or being negotiated, ensure the covenants and clauses are reviewed thoroughly. Every loan, equity investment or financing facility will differ significantly. Business circumstances can change rapidly so you want to have "seen" some of the potential by modeling in your own business results.

It may be possible to request including terms or clauses in the agreements that give the company options.

- From the best case scenario consider including options to repay the funds, terminate the agreement, or convert the debt earlier than the maturity or repayment date if that would be beneficial (in some situations it is more advantageous to keep the facility unchanged for the full contract term).

- From the worst case scenario "forewarned is forearmed" so know the parameters of where the company must operate in order to stay on-side the covenants and hence assess the risk and consequences to the company if the facility is called, foreclosed, or even becomes punitive.

   If actual results start to look less than favorable management can move to more frequent short term cash forecasts and carefully conserve cash. This will ensure operations do continue until more cash becomes available and/or sales generate sufficient cash to allow for a reduced review frequency.

Varying and customizing the terms of a loan is not always possible, but it may be beneficial to request changes, depending on the nature of the instrument and the funds provider.

Remember that unforeseen circumstances happen without warning and in many cases are entirely outside of the control of the company (think economic, health or environmental catastrophes, acts of God, etc.). When a legal contract is in place the clauses stand and your company needs to know what could be managed by management when things go wrong, or go really well.

If the agreement has been modeled, and is reviewed periodically in future budget periods, management remains consistently informed and can actively manage all outcomes for the best of the company.

Never allow lack of information or vigilance, on either carefully reviewing draft agreements or on managing existing agreements, to amplify risk for your company.

Funding Comes in Many Forms

There are many sources of funding but the costs and availability can vary significantly dependent on the type, the lenders or investors, terms and security of the instruments, and on general economic conditions at the time of negotiation.

The primary variations are:

- Equity or debt, or a hybrid of the two,
- With or without very restrictive or specific terms and covenants,
- Require security or unsecured,
- Repayable or not,
- Convertible or not between debt and equity, or an alternative instrument,
- Interest, or return, bearing or interest free,
- Require scheduled reporting to the funds provider or not,
- Public or private sources,
- Public or private markets and disclosures,
- Require additional "related" instruments or not,

- Supplied by government backed or private funders,
- Short or long term funding period.

The process of soliciting, negotiating and securing the funds is usually time consuming so do not wait until desperate. Try to secure funding or at least the facility when *not* required yet.

Be conservative in operating and in negotiating – always hope for the best but plan for the absolute worst. That way it is unlikely the business will suffer catastrophic consequences if something does not go fully to plan.

Get creative when possible. Do not take the easiest and first offer presented to you. There may be more alternatives to consider and often considering a "combination" of types of funding sources and providers, and alternatives on security, will give the best result for both the company and the funders.

Diversify funding sources. Just like with diversifying business strategies or products sold, diversification in funding

- Is less risky and allows management to better weather potential downturns.
- Improves the chances of securing the appropriate financing, flexibility in terms that are customized to the specific circumstances, and the most effective available security.
- Is a demonstration to lenders that your management team is proactive and creative.

Each of the primary categories of equity, bank loans, angel investors, government grants, private loans, and business incubators have specific advantages and disadvantages as well as criteria used in their evaluation of the business.

Most Common Categories of Funding

1. Personal investment

The first investor in a new business and often the ongoing investor in a family or entrepreneurial business, is usual closely related to the founder(s) (their own cash or with collateral on personal assets) which demonstrate long-term commitment and willingness to take risks.

2. Patient capital

Money loaned by a spouse, parents, family or friends is usually patient as it is repaid when the business profits increase.

Factors to consider:
- Family and friends rarely have substantial capital
- They may want equity in the business
- A business relationship with family or friends can be, or become, very complicated.

3. Venture capital

An equity investor (frequently a fund) that invests in a company (frequently technology-driven or at least has high growth potential in sectors like information technology and biotechnology) that exhibits high growth potential and often when it requires financing to get established in its market.

It may be start-up funding or expansion funding where the private company does not have access to more public equity markets.

The venture capitalist expects a high return on their investment, which is often generated when the business starts selling shares to the public. The company and management derive most value when the investors bring relevant experience and knowledge to the business.

4. Angel investment

Angels are generally wealthy individuals or their personal companies who invest directly in small companies and contribute their experience, network of contacts, technical and/or management knowledge.

Angel investments are frequently smaller than venture capitalists, may take the form of equity or convertible debt, often have funding terms that are more favourable than those of other lenders, and their goal is often to help the business get established and to support the entrepreneur behind the business, not just the business itself. The capital is frequently unsecured, and the angel has a clear exit strategies for ending involvement with the business.

The angel usually has a seat on the board of directors and the company gives an assurance of transparency, but many angels keep a low profile.

5. Business incubators

Business incubators (or "accelerators") generally focus on the high-tech sector or economic development in an area (usually geographic, a city or region) by providing support for new businesses in various stages of development. Commonly, incubators invite businesses to share their premises, as well as administrative, logistical and/or technical resources. For example, an incubator might share the use of laboratories so that a new business can develop and test its products less expensively before beginning production. Generally, the incubation phase lasts a few years and once the product is ready, the business leaves the incubator's premises to enter its industrial production phase. Businesses that receive this kind of support often operate within state-of-the-art sectors such as biotechnology, information technology, multimedia, or industrial technology.

6. Government grants and subsidies

Government agencies provide financing such as grants and subsidies that may be available to a business within the prioritized industry or area of focus.

There usually is significant competition for the grants and subsidies, and the criteria for awards are often stringent. Terms differ depending on the granting agency and focus area. Most match funds that the company raises from another source e.g. may require that the identified project or research is funded 50% internally and 50% by the grant, or 40:60, and some will only fund expenditure meeting specific criteria (e.g. purchases within certain industries or certain countries, only equipment and not people cost, etc.). The grants or subsidies will be obtained by submitting an application (in a prescribed form) with a detailed justification, work plans, expertise of key managers, etc. and after the award there are ongoing reporting requirements that compare actual results to those plans.

For the right projects, grants and subsidies are well worth the effort to apply for them and track the spending.

Alternative to a grant: Certain research and development expenditure may qualify for special taxation allowances. The allowances can be generous and are worth considering. Some allow for claiming more than 100% of the cash cost so the cash flow impact is largely or entirely neutralized. The same expenditure items can normally not be claimed for both the taxation allowance and a grant or subsidy funding.

7. Bank loans

Bank loans are the most commonly used source of funding for small and medium-sized businesses. Banks offer different advantages, whether it is personalized service or customized repayment, online or in person, conservative or creative, different costs and terms, variations in security, or postponement of the principal payments.

A disadvantage is that many large commercial banks focus on companies with a sound track record and have excellent credit ratings, thus are less helpful for entrepreneurial or new business. Many loans require a personal guarantee from the entrepreneurs but there are also alternative funding options available when a government agency (or similar independent government backed entity) is willing to provide a loan guarantee or when alternative security can be accepted.

No One-size-fits-all

The funding options, sources of funding, terms of funds, restrictions, advantages and disadvantages, are many and varied.

There is absolutely no one-size-fits-all, it is a complex area but can be handled by most senior management.

The earlier a business considers this topic and works to evaluate the need, the options available, and the best fit for the specific circumstances the more beneficial and the greater the likelihood of finding an excellent solution. There are many ways to get assistance in identifying alternatives and your financial executive, chief financial officer and/or a funding agent should be able to assist.

Avoid a Limiting Factor

Do not allow funds to become a limiting factor in running, growing and strategically pivoting a thriving, profitable business.

It will not be if

- Cash availability is considered to be one of the strategic enablers to actively manage and leverage on the road to success, and
- Management considers cash forecasting and cash management to be an important function within the company.

Funds and funding can be an emotional and intimidating topic because of the variety, complexity and especially the significant cost when things go wrong. There are many horror stories but also many phenomenal successes when business strategy is enabled by optimal cash flexibility.

Finance, cash flows, and funds flexibility are among the most critical areas in the ongoing success and existence of every company.

Get It Right:

- Forecast cash needs right,
- Negotiate facilities terms and flexibility right,
- Manage and use cash right,
- Redeem or convert facilities at the right time, and
- Consider getting assistance from the right support and advisors when uncertain.

One of the tests of leadership is the ability to recognize a problem before it becomes an emergency.
Arnold H. Glasow

Luck is what happens when preparation meets opportunity.
Seneca, Roman Philosopher

NOTES

Chapter 5

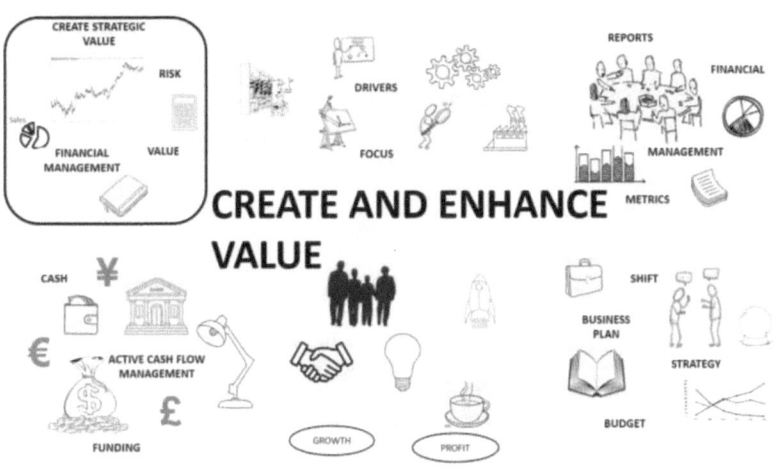

Financial Management – Creative Value

Why Disciplined and Creative Financial Management is Important

Financial management is the art and science of adding value, minimizing cost and managing risk; including directing and managing business support services at optimal cost with effective control so that the company can meet its goals.

The functions include a range of corporate, legal, statutory, compliance and taxation requirements that are transactional, administrative, professional and technical in nature.

All business decisions have financial consequences and the person or team managing the finance must oversee systems and processes to:

- Ensure risk exposures are managed,

- Ensure the financial data is prepared and analyzed accurately, and with insight,
- Monitor and manage the firm's financial status internally and externally, and
- Partner to identify and deliver value.

The investment in quality financial management delivers returns across the company.

Primary Responsibility and Resources

The primary areas of financial management focus will be:

- Corporate services – overall company policy and strategy, governance, company culture, and communication with (or management of) investors, lenders and stakeholders.

  Internal controls, policies and procedures, public disclosures or external reporting, investor relations, and board governance are some of the tasks.

- Financial shared services – transactional, administration and compliance (legal, statutory, taxation) support.

  These include accounting and transaction tasks, taxation, legal, compliance with regulations, and general administration. Compliance with generally accepted accounting principles (GAAP), Sarbanes Oxley or the equivalent (SOX), and laws and regulations related to employment, privacy, security, licensing are usually included.

- Financial planning, reporting, and decision support:
  - Preparing the financial plan (forecast finance needs and sources over a given period).
  - Investing the business funds in projects, assets and business transactions that provide the best returns in relation to their risks.
  - Obtaining funding for the operations and investments, with the best balance between debt and

equity, and managing the way cash is used and collected.

The company's financial management will use their experience to tie the parts together, help manage the company to the planned future, and interpret the financial consequences one event or action may have in another area.

Highly focused growth companies (unless large) frequently appoint financial team members responsible for the transactions as employees and use external part-time consultants as senior expertise. They find it gives a combination of the best expertise at an appropriate cost. The executive brings experience in senior or complex matters at a manageable cost and the transaction team is available for ongoing tasks and projects.

The best senior managers spend a large portion of their time (especially in smaller companies) teaching, mentoring and coaching managers and staff. They work to enhance value by growing internal capability and ensuring the team can make the best decisions for the company as a whole.

Enhance Value in Diverse Areas

In addition to accounting, financial management, reporting, and strategic planning experience the diverse financial officer will have experience to:

- Assist in reviewing and drafting contracts,
- Assist in human resources and people management,
- Manage investor or public relations,
- Manage compliance with regulations that the company may need to consider,
- Identify risks to which the company is or may become exposed, and manage or advise on risk mitigation,
- Predict and interpret the impact that agreements or contracts being considered may have; especially where the contract requires a major strategic or administrative change, and

- Explore and implement appropriate systems and technology to:
    - Enhance the efficiency of the company, and
    - Facilitate rapid planning, setting of new targets and revision of models and dashboards as the company growth continues or assumptions and inputs change.

Facilitate Nimble Change

As the company succeeds and grows it will have a need to become increasingly nimble and strategic in management and business planning. It may be appropriate at this time to consider enhanced systems and processes to facilitate the efficiency, but there may be no need. The financial officer will assist with fact-based evaluation to enable the decision.

Are New Systems Required?

Some executives consider enterprise resource planning (ERP) and business intelligence (BI) systems to be "accounting systems". This is unfortunate as the systems offer significantly more value than pure accounting.

These systems house a wealth of business intelligence because they have information from across all business areas. They are a valuable tools for easily and regularly delivering key performance metrics, management report information, budgeting and strategic plans (including scenario "what if" options), etc.

It may be necessary to move from the initial bookkeeping, accounting, and operational information systems and processes as the company grows. But it may be entirely unnecessary. Many of the modern systems can efficiently and inexpensively "bridge" between systems and delay (or avoid) the need to convert in a "big bang" that can be very disruptive, and frequently expensive.

Your financial management will advise whether business intelligence systems can work with data currently available or which system areas to upgrade as a priority.

Moving towards a single, unified system or data warehouse will provide better analytical tools to leverage the intellectual capital of the business. The involvement of financial management in the decision will ensure the value of the contribution and potential improvement in the decision making process is assessed.

Major Strategic Initiatives

Experienced chief financial officers will assist on acquisitions, disposals, restructuring, and other pivot events. These may be the highly effective way management has identified for enhancing the value of the company.

The options need to be considered with as much strategic thought and evaluation of facts as any other plans, and care must be taken to avoid emotion in the process. Many of the strategic events will require the company to achieve, or at least move towards:

- Certifications,
- Financial and/or social and strategic audits,
- Environmental, social and governance (ESG) reporting and certifications,
- Alternative corporate structures or formation,
- Listing on public markets like major stock exchanges,
- Verification of internal security and practices such as privacy and confidentiality of information, information technology and cyber security.

These bring additional cost to be factored into the deal evaluation but may themselves also contribute significant value.

Creative Value by Financial Management?

The financial management has a key role in creatively driving and facilitating business value creation. This includes quality of earnings and transformation of the business.

Hold on ... creative!? ... Are accountants and financial managers creative?

There are two major methods of growing value:

1. Financial restructuring
2. Growing economic performance.

1. Financial Restructuring

Because of the financial management's view into the operation of all areas of the business (and any acquisitions, disposals or corporate changes) they have the opportunity to play a lead role in creating value through "financial restructuring".

Financial restructuring may be:

- Increasing the focus of the business on what is most important and delivering most value in the current products sold, activities, business locations, etc.

- Identifying areas of waste or ways of doing things better. Perhaps disciplines and practices from one area of the business can be introduced to another? Or resource allocation between business units, divisions, or other parts of the business can be improved.

- Alerting managers to the marginal or subtle value derived from improving each of the activities that contribute to performance. This may include realigning the operating units of the business for a better fit with the rest of the organization. All parts of the business need to work together within a single strategic framework or service delivery chain and the finance function can help with oversight, coordination or reporting.

- In appropriate circumstances, considering shared services and transfer pricing to better leverage the resources of the business and reduce redundancy.

The financial manager can creatively contribute significant value.

2. Ongoing Economic Value Generation

Economic Performance Reviewed

In addition to analyzing and reporting on the accounting performance of the business, financial management can assist in understanding the components of true, or "economic", performance.

Accounting performance (as measured in the official financial statements) is important for many reasons but the economic performance reports the *total value* of the business. It looks at results (especially cash returns) and performance of the assets, liabilities and overall market strength. It also has a longer-term payoff and ongoing exponential impact.

How do you see it?

To review the economic performance of the company look at the results and consider investments made in future performance (example, accounting performance may expense education or new product development, but economic performance considers the value it creates in future returns). So it looks at the *quality* of earnings which drives the overall value of the business.

Many intangibles that are important to value-creation are not included on the balance sheet. These may be the value in the company's team of people, new ideas from research projects, the technology, innovative marketing, key strategic partners or suppliers, certifications to install products, patents, etc.

Measure non-financial parts

Management must identify the strengths and weaknesses of the business and try to measure the non-financial parts that are major elements of value-creation, or at least consider the value it contributes to future accounting returns.

A single, unified system or data warehouse and developing better analytical tools can help to more quickly and efficiently drill into the most important kernels of fact, improve decision-making and leverage the intellectual capital that are the specific value behind the company.

It is necessary to balance financial forms of measurement with non-financial forms of measurement. Quality financial management will assist.

Value Based Management

The mandate for creating value, and hence a valuable successful company, is to invest in assets that provide returns higher than the cost of capital.

The assets may be tangible and intangible. The people are potentially the most valuable; they have and create ideas that are potential assets to be invested in. Each company must invest its limited time and resources wisely to create value.

Changing the entire business to think value-creation is challenging because it is a different mindset. Most companies and people have traditionally been driven by profits. But with some perseverance and ensuring everyone understands the difference between growing on profit alone or on increasing aspects of value (which expands wealth for everyone), everyone can become enthusiastic and successful.

Without the effort to explain the difference and that profit is one component of value, the process can become frustrating and demotivate team members.

Moving to Value Based Management

Successful value based management requires:

(1) Driven by the Chief Executive Officer and senior management who are fully committed.

(2) Cross Functional Team: Since value based management involves the whole business it is most effective to have a cross-functional team lead the change, encourage communication, design how value based management can work in each part of the company, and resolve differences when they arise.

Most companies that have transformed to be more value based start by:

- Benchmarking their value-creation against the competition (if possible and if desired),
- Making distinctions between
    - efficient capital (capital that is under their control and is generating returns higher than the cost of the capital),
    - capital not controlled (capital not under company control and hence not managed) and
    - underperforming capital (capital under company control but not earning an adequate return).
- Driving the value initiatives from the strategic plan, which then determines the operating and investment decisions. The efficient and underperforming capital is all managed for performance enhancement that drives growth in value.

The initial evaluation creates a starting point and the company can then move forward and evaluate the "value generated" each time a decision is made, a financial or performance result is evaluated, or an opportunity for change or growth is presented.

How to Assess Value Increased by Value Based Management?

If it is possible to accurately measure the value of the company (in a public company it is easiest as it has a share price), it is possible to also calculate the overall value added by all of the actions taken in a given period. But that total value is not always as easy to determine in a private company (or during periods when the public share price is impacted by general market factors), and it is not usually a good use of funds to have the company professionally valued on a regular basis.

The market value added could be calculated as the difference between the capital that has been invested (in cash i.e. excluding potential distortion from accounting entries) and the market value of the capital. (When the company is funded by both debt and equity the value of the debt must be deducted from the total company value to determine the equity value.)

So value added is the net present value of the return that all investments made by the company are expected to deliver in the future.

Value added over a defined period would then be current value less value at an earlier time.

If the market value cannot be independently determined companies use a variety of methods to approximate the value of the contribution an asset will make.

It does not have to be entirely accurate for use in internal evaluations as long as the company uses a consistent approach each time. They can make comparisons or ensure the return on a purchase, new investment initiative, etc. or even from an asset, product line, etc. that is to be discontinued, will produce a greater value "after" than it did "before".

Generating Value through Activity

One example of a way business value is generated is by getting one thing right in the operations most of the time; in this way companies gain a competitive advantage that becomes a significant source of value.

For many companies, this involves things like

1. Higher Quality - Producing an exceptionally high quality product.
2. Customer Service - Delivering products and services (and related documentation) to customers with speed, solving the customer's problem effectively, possessing knowledge about the customer for better service, etc.
3. Continuous Improvement - Constantly looking for ways to improve internal processes of the business as well as the product and/or service delivered to customers.
4. Lower Prices - Delivering products and services at the lowest possible price in a highly competitive marketplace.

Creating value is the reward an organization receives when it does the thing consistently well. Well-managed companies pay close attention to these sources of value.

People Create Exponential Value

The old approach to creating value was to reorganize the parts of the company and/or cut costs (often unscrupulously across the board without considering consequences in other areas) but this seldom contributes lasting value. Especially if done mainly for that purpose.

A focus on people and empowering them to create value is sustainable and usually creates processes of exponential value creation.

Innovative strategies are created by people but the challenge is to get everyone engaged in a conversation about the business and strategies. Some companies have succeeded by making everyone a shareholder; they think differently about the business.

All of the other elements of value-creation (such as financial restructurings, excellent product quality, efficiency in operations, etc.) have limitations on how much value can be generated over the long run but innovative strategizing is perpetual and continuous. When people are engaged and want to create value they repeatedly identify ways to do so. It is an integral part of value-creation and as a result, innovative strategizing is the most important element of exponential value-creation

Engage the Full Business Team to Grow Value

Creative, strategic, forward-looking financial management may the secret behind the growth and success of many companies. The chief financial officer can partner with senior management to increased returns, foresee and avoid (or minimize) strategic risks, mentor and train employees, and in the process increase corporate value.

Financial management creates value in the company by having the best *business people*, not by having the best accountants. Accounting and technical skills are a given, the forward thinking valuable managers contribute value well beyond.

Statistics have shown that four in five companies fail because they run out of cash or stop generating value. If management and the founders wish to keep having fun in the business and operating for years one of the best ways is a focus on financial management to deliver value.

Management is about persuading people to do things they do not want to do, while leadership is about inspiring people to do things they never thought they could.
Steve Jobs

NOTES

Chapter 6

Business Success, Value and Profit IS Fun

Congratulations! You have made it through the entire book and now have all of the tools to successfully and rapidly grow your company and dramatically increase the value of both the company, and the products and services you deliver to customers.

You and your team know to

- Focus on your key business drivers and accordingly effortlessly manage the most important aspects.
- Achieve exactly what your business planned, through the nearer term details of your strategic plan and budget.
- Fully utilize the assistance and skills of your financial management to ensure you deliver value from every aspect of the business activities.
- Use specifically tailored and regularly discussed financial

and management reports to confirm and correct course (or amplify achievements when possible). And

- Leverage growth with the best sources of financing available.

The clarity and consistency of purpose ensure that your employee and management teams are synchronized in their approach to all business decisions, that profitability and return to stakeholders will expand, and consequently that your business is supreme and unrivaled.

Because your company is funded in a timely manner and working on realistic, although visionary, goals with an enthusiastic, fully empowered team your management will be free to undertake strategic growth, creative research and development, and become an industry leader.

Your business certainly is *not* on course to become a name on the list of failed or discontinued businesses.

Take Advantage of Changes in Economic and Business Environments

Changes in business environments and economic changes have an impact on all companies.

For your business these are most likely to provide opportunities for success; it is unlikely the impact would be catastrophic as your company receives early warning through the drivers and regular reports. You are in a position to pivot when changes are required and reinvent for new circumstances. The enthusiasm and involvement of the employees is likely to create business value and allow them to contribute ideas and alternatives to make your company a leader.

The strategic tools and partnership with empowered, capable and enthusiastic team members becomes the secret weapon that ensures vigilance and success.

Harness Energy and Achieve Success

The industry, regulations, maturity of the technology or other factors specific to your company may have a significant impact on the timelines of success but once the model is set it will become a self-renewing process.

Harness the energy of a team that continually fine-tunes operations, remains alert for opportunities or changes, and rises to meet challenges. The team spirit is the energy behind the business success, increasing profitability and creating cash flows. The support mechanism now implemented keeps the team informed with a minimum of effort and thus immediately alert when action is required.

The tools create a stable springboard for exponential growth, save measureable amounts of management time, and at the same time inject fun and team-spirit into the business achievements.

Society is richer with diverse choice, your company is a role model of corporate success, and the positive internal atmosphere creates a "good place to work" culture. There truly are many beneficiaries, not least of which are the corporate shareholders.

Value in Deliberate Discipline

As one last technique to round out exceptional growth, ensure you harness the value of your shared services (administration, accounting, human resource, information technology, etc.).

Invest in appropriate technology and security, and dedicate time and effort to standardize systems, process, and procedures.

If the customer-facing and operational functions efficiently partner with your administrative or back-office teams to:

- Create one integrated service delivery chain,
- Streamline processes,
- Add automation to reduce workload and provide immediate feedback,

It removes significant cost, generates value and further contributes to the corporate growth cycle.

The most important part is that your customers will be thrilled with their experience, which is the best sales and marketing technique available.

Can you Start Now?

The only thing that remains now is for you to put the ideas into action. Promise you will take one action to start the growth and value chain …. Now!

Remember that the tools may be used individually or in combination, the most value is derived when all are in use but with every action taken and every tool implemented you will see and feel an impact. The effect is cumulative so the more you achieve, the more value you will derive.

Perfection

Do not attempt to adopt a perfection approach.

Start somewhere and plan to iterate until you achieve your personalized optimal solution. The tools work best when well customized to your own business and management style so choose one task to try, and do it. There is little risk of failure.

There are only a few reasons people fail to implement new techniques or improvements:

    a. Analysis paralysis – there is limited value in trying to learn increasingly more before starting. All that happens is that you get stuck chasing bright shiny objects (or squirrels) in the hope of achieving perfection the first time. There is no perfection until you try, and successful business people have a bias for action.

    b. Reluctance or inability to delegate – involve members of your employee and management team. Business is a team sport and the most efficient way to reach the best is to harness the energy, ideas and expertise of them all. It is not possible or advisable for the chief executive or founder to be involved in or oversee every action taken or meeting attended in the company; delegate appropriately, let your team surprise you and optimize cost.

  c. Being different – your business and group of people absolutely is different, and that is exactly why you need to make a start. Refine and tweak as you find alternatives and improvements suitable for your specific genius and style. These tools have worked in many businesses and across many countries. There is no value in trying to determine why these *will not* work for your business; try them so you can experience value.

The world needs more entrepreneurs, successful business people and successful companies; do not deprive the world of your contribution.

Your ultimate competitive advantage is in anticipating change and taking appropriate action. You deserve business success and it is attainable so build an extraordinary business, have the consequent fun, remove complexity from your management process and trigger the exponential growth you deserve.

There is a powerful driving force inside every human being that, once unleashed, can make any vision, dream, or desire a reality.
Anthony Robbin

If you don't understand the details of your business you are going to fail.
Jeff Bezos

NOTES

Chapter Afterword

TOP 10 ERRORS THAT PREVENT BOTTOM LINE GROWTH

(Usually Blamed on "The Economy", "Circumstance" or "Bad Luck")

1. Failing to practice precise cash flow optimization.
2. Random acts of change or course correction without effective analysis or adequate implementation.
3. Not identifying and using accurate drivers, and failing to refine to perfect them.
4. Not reviewing both progress and plans, and the linkage between them.
5. Running out of cash due to reacting too late, or not raising funding with adequate lead time.
6. Not developing strength, depth and value in management of the company finance.

7. Allowing analysis paralysis to delay or prevent optimizing and driving your company success.
8. Reviewing results, charts, plans and projections too infrequently, or not understanding the messages.
9. Not identifying and using the perfect resource or person for the task, especially when expert skill or experience is required.
10. Not fully engaging the entire team in order to leverage performance, passion and success.

STEPS YOU WILL TAKE TO RESTART YOUR BOTTOM LINE GROWTH

1. _____
2. _____
3. _____
4. _____
5. _____
6. _____
7. _____
8. _____
9. _____
10. _____
11. _____
12. _____
13. _____
14. _____
15. _____

Next Steps

I hope this book has sparked some new thinking and insights for you. Whenever you're ready, here are three options to help increase your success:

1. Subscribe to the Business Growth Focus podcast. https://proteaconsulting.ca/podcast

2. Download a copy of the Financial Growth Scorecard to assess your current status and what to work on next. https://proteaconsulting.ca/growth

3. Work with Protea Consulting Professional Corporation, Chartered Professional Accountant, to achieve the growth and success your company is truly capable of. To find out if we're a fit, email me at info@proteaconsulting.ca "1-on-1" in the subject line.

About the Author

Nola Heale founded Protea Consulting Professional Corporation, Chartered Professional Accountant, to work with successful clients to enhance their bottom line and prosperity through financial oversight, efficiency, and streamlined processes. She has experience in very small owner-managed businesses to vast international public companies, and has worked across two continents. From manufacturing, mining, health services, oilfield services, power generation, utilities, intermodal transportation and warehousing, to aerospace technology she has proved that bottom lines can be grown in any economic conditions.

For more information, contact Nola at https://proteaconsulting.ca/contact or info@proteaconsulting.ca

www.ingramcontent.com/pod-product-compliance
Lightning Source LLC
Chambersburg PA
CBHW031442210526
45464CB00005B/2308